TCHAIKOVSKY'S THE NUTCRACKER

CLARINET

TITLE	PAGE NUMBER

To access audio visit:
www.halleonard.com/mylibrary
Enter Code
2002-8508-8977-9384

Arranged and Recorded by Donald Sosin

HOW TO USE THE AUDIO ACCOMPANIMENT
A melody cue appears on the right channel only. If your stereo or computer has a balance adjustment, you can adjust the volume of the melody by turning down the right channel.

ISBN 978-1-57560-960-7

Visit Hal Leonard Online at
www.halleonard.com

OVERTURE

By Pyotr Il'yich Tchaikovsky

CLARINET

Allegro giusto ♩ = 100

MARCH

By Pyotr Il'yich Tchaikovsky

CLARINET

SPANISH DANCE
("Chocolate")

By Pyotr Il'yich Tchaikovsky

CLARINET

ARABIAN DANCE
("Coffee")

By Pyotr Il'yich Tchaikovsky

CLARINET

Comodo ♩. = 100

CHINESE DANCE
("Tea")

By Pyotr Il'yich Tchaikovsky

CLARINET

Allegro moderato ♩ = 130
Orch.
Play
mf
3

RUSSIAN DANCE
(Trepak)

By Pyotr Il'yich Tchaikovsky

CLARINET

Molto vivace ♩ = 128
Play
mf

DANCE OF THE REED FLUTES

By Pyotr Il'yich Tchaikovsky

CLARINET

To Coda
sim.
D.S. al Coda
Coda

WALTZ OF THE FLOWERS

By Pyotr Il'yich Tchaikovsky

CLARINET

DANCE OF THE SUGARPLUM FAIRY

By Pyotr Il'yich Tchaikovsky

CLARINET

FINAL WALTZ AND APOTHEOSIS

By Pyotr Il'yich Tchaikovsky

CLARINET

Coda
1.
2.